Guest Book
Tiffany Blue Edition

By

Matthew Harper

www.matthewharper.info

Guests

Names	Thoughts

Thank You

Names   Thoughts

Thank You

Guests

Names   *Thoughts*

Thank You

Guests

Names   Thoughts

Thank You

Guests

Names   Thoughts

Thank You

Guests

Names   Thoughts

Thank You

Guests

Names	Thoughts

Thank You

Guests

Names   Thoughts

Thank You

Guests

Names　　　　　　　　　　　　Thoughts

Thank You

Guests

Names	Thoughts

Thank You

Guests

Names   Thoughts

Thank You

Guests

Names	Thoughts

Thank You

Guests

Names   Thoughts

Thank You

Guests

Names   Thoughts

Thank You

Guests

Names · Thoughts

Thank You

Guests

Names   Thoughts

Thank You

Guests

Names   Thoughts

Thank You

Guests

Names Thoughts

Thank You

Guests

Names	Thoughts

Thank You

Guests

Names Thoughts

Thank You

Guests

Names　　　　　　　　　　Thoughts

Thank You

Guests

Names Thoughts

Thank You

Guests

Names   Thoughts

Thank You

Guests

Names	Thoughts

Thank You

Guests

Names   *Thoughts*

Thank You

Guests

Names	Thoughts

Thank You

Guests

Names   Thoughts

Thank You

Guests

Names   *Thoughts*

Thank You

Guests

Names   *Thoughts*

Thank You

Guests

Names   Thoughts

Thank You

Guests

Names   *Thoughts*

Thank You

Guests

Names　　　　　　　　　　　　　　　Thoughts

Thank You

Guests

Names	Thoughts

Thank You

Guests

Names   Thoughts

Thank You

Guests

Names   *Thoughts*

Thank You

Guests

Names   Thoughts

Thank You

Guests

Names   *Thoughts*

Thank You

Guests

Names   Thoughts

Thank You

Guests

Names	Thoughts

Thank You

Guests

Names   Thoughts

Thank You

Guests

Names   Thoughts

Thank You

Guests

Names · Thoughts

Thank You

Guests

Names	Thoughts

Thank You

Guests

Names   Thoughts

Thank You

Guests

Names	Thoughts

Thank You

Guests

Names Thoughts

Thank You

Names   Thoughts

Thank You

Guests

Names   Thoughts

Thank You

Guests

Names   *Thoughts*

Thank You

Guests

    Names   Thoughts

Thank You

Guests

Names   Thoughts

Thank You

Guests

Names   Thoughts

Thank You

Guests

Names   Thoughts

Thank You

Guests

Names   Thoughts

Thank You

Guests

Names　　　　　　　　　Thoughts

Thank You

Guests

Names   *Thoughts*

Thank You

Guests

Names   Thoughts

Thank You

Guests

Names	Thoughts

Thank You

Guests

Names	Thoughts

Thank You

Guests

Names   Thoughts

Thank You

Guests

Names	Thoughts

Thank You

Guests

Names	Thoughts

Thank You

Guests

Names   *Thoughts*

Thank You

Guests

Names   Thoughts

Thank You

Guests

Names   Thoughts

Thank You

Guests

Names　　　　　　　　　　　　Thoughts

Thank You

Guests

Names ### Thoughts

Thank You

Guests

Names   Thoughts

Thank You

Guests

Names   Thoughts

Thank You

Guests

Names   Thoughts

Thank You

Guests

Names　　　　　　　　　　　　　Thoughts

Thank You

Guests

Names	Thoughts

Thank You

Guests

Names	Thoughts

Thank You

Guests

Names	Thoughts

Thank You

Guests

Names   Thoughts

Thank You

Guests

Names	Thoughts

Thank You

Guests

Names	Thoughts

Thank You

Guests

Names   *Thoughts*

Thank You

Guests

Names   Thoughts

Thank You

Names   Thoughts

Thank You

Guests

Names   **Thoughts**

Thank You

Guests

Names	Thoughts

Thank You

Guests

Names   Thoughts

Thank You

Guests

Names	Thoughts

Thank You

Guests

Names   Thoughts

Thank You

Guests

Names Thoughts

Thank You

Guests

Names   Thoughts

Thank You

Guests

Names   **Thoughts**

Thank You

Guests

Names	Thoughts

Thank You

Guests

Names   Thoughts

Thank You

Guests

Names   Thoughts

Thank You

Guests

Names   Thoughts

Thank You

Guests

Names   Thoughts

Thank You

Guests

Names	Thoughts

Thank You

Guests

Names	Thoughts

Thank You

Guests

Names	Thoughts

Thank You

Guests

Names	Thoughts

Thank You

Guests

Names   Thoughts

Thank You

Guests

Names   Thoughts

Thank You

Guests

Names	Thoughts

Thank You

Guests

Names   Thoughts

Thank You

Guests

Names	Thoughts

Thank You

Guests

NamesThoughts

Thank You

Guests

Names *Thoughts*

Thank You

Made in the USA
Lexington, KY
07 February 2017